FINISHING LINE PRESS

www.finishinglinepress.com

WILD CANVAS

poems by

Alison Davis

Finishing Line Press
Georgetown, Kentucky

WILD CANVAS

ACKNOWLEDGMENTS

"Bloodlines" was published in *The Central Dissent* through *New Plains Review*.

Publisher: Leah Huete de Maines
Editor: Christen Kincaid
Cover Art: Kamden Davis
Author Photo: Tony Davis
Cover Design: Elizabeth Maines McCleavy

Order online: www.finishinglinepress.com
also available on amazon.com

Author inquiries and mail orders:
Finishing Line Press
PO Box 1626
Georgetown, Kentucky 40324
USA

Contents

DRAFT: HOW TO OVERCOME WRITER'S BLOCK (v. 16)

have you tried writing with your feet? the alphabet is
different that way, it's jagged and pregnant or
unrecognizable and commanding
such that the letters mean something else to you
what you already know is obscured so that the S can
speak
and slither
and show you that you are just a hair's width from the shorthand for infinity
turned up on its side

don't read a book that's for sure certainly other's words will
seem so pretty and polished and you will forget how
the tides had their way with them for years,
thus avoid wrongly wishing you would be washed out right now to that place
where the meaning is
because you will resurface and cough up nothing but foam
the sunken ships can't be reached this way and we "came to explore the wreck"

take out a map if you dare but only if it's accordion-style cumbersome and you
could never fold
it back up the way it was when you first handled it
that's the kind of paths we chart with words, all unfolding and changing creases
and
rearranging what is face to face and back to back until
the front turns up again up but the insides got lost on their way to a destination
that was never meant for them
imagine the places instead, what kind of fountain stands in that town square
and how many children toss their pennies in while mothers scold
hurry up
and if the first rain drop falls on the lip or on the
turbid surface

write it anyway even if it means nothing
especially if it means nothing
and of course don't erase a thing
like you're talking on the phone to a friend but back in the day when fingers and
cords were made for each other for twirling and enveloping and embracing
write it just like that the paper is your friend on the other end of the line and the
words can't be
deleted
or scratched out

and even if you feel like saying i'm sorry the connection isn't so strong in a small
irresolute voice
you don't have to
just keep the conversation going

because poems are for you they feed you you deserve to be at the head
of the table
and taking seconds first this time
and the servings are just mashed words and sauteed verbs but they
fill the utilitarian room with the redolence of spices and taste like
truth
truth doesn't have to be gourmet focus instead on all the fixings
but if you still feel like you need a recipe maybe consult
a Roget's or a Merriam one more time

don't try to make it too clean

starting and finishing are closer than they seem

SOME MORE URGENT THAN OTHERS

Are there any common birth defects in soldier beetles?
Which of my neighbors is always practicing the flute
from seven to eight in the morning? How hot is too
hot? What were you dreaming about during the Great

Conjunction of 2020, and did it come true for you
like it did for me? Can what these people say and what
those people say ever be reconciled? Is there a more
elegant way to slow down a reader than by *using italics*?

How many times must I bow down to be completely
beheaded? Why are we so keen on the Pythagorean Theorem
but dismiss his views on the immortality of souls as
hopelessly misguided? If this poem contained a set of

compassion imperatives (such as: mail someone a handwritten
thank you card; scatter wildflower seeds in a median; stand
at the door for as long as it takes to hold it open for twenty-
three people; forgive yourself for that mistake you made—

yes, that one—when you were too young to know better;
kiss a tree, a flower, and a hand), would you do them?
Why do I still keep picking up every feather that I see, even
the spindly ones caked with dirt? Did the nurse cry when

she got home that evening? Who else can feel the Crown of Thorns
in their prickling sweat while climbing a steep hill? Which
of the Greek words for love is most appropriate here?
Is it time to tell the truth yet? How many Kaw River tributaries

have I dipped my toes in, and how long before the next flood?
Does he keep in touch with anyone from his cell block? What if we
changed the name from tinnitus to detecting the music of the spheres?
Could this vibration triangulating its way through my body be

what Galway Kinnell meant about hearing your *whole existence*?

BERRY PICKING

My daughters rush toward
the thicket, arms outstretched,
a cry of joy that starts
in their hearts moves up through
their eyes and pours out of their mouths.
They snap the blackberries
from their prickly stems, push back
the thorny tangles in search of more
Sweetness. I watch the juice stain
their fingers, lips, drip down their
chins. The palette of their childhood,
The wild canvas of skin.
Will they remember how beautiful
they were, made up in summer's colors,
how brilliant and good their bodies were
on the side of the busy road, lost in
these fleshy fruits? The sky their only
mirror, their reflections vast and
untamed. When one day their friends, surely
just a few short revolutions from now,
want to meet at the drugstore to
hold up lipsticks and cheek rouge against
their searching faces, will they know
what perfection they came from? Will the
the scratch of brambles on their bodies
still call to them like a treasure map
they want to follow? Will the summer sap
of childhood have run dry?

For now, they sing
          give thanks to the Mother Gaia
and laugh in the face of
all these mysteries.

FAR FROM HOME

My mother drove fourteen hours
to cut her father's fingernails and tell
stories about the last time they danced
the polka and ate dill pickle soup.
The framed photographs
on the wall will keep their shape
much longer than any of our bodies.
For months, my father turned his mother over
in the twin bed, just off from the kitchen,
and readied himself to change the sheets.
Water was pouring from her legs, a rare
but possible condition, like living. They never
put her in a home because they were brave
enough to befriend the end. And here we are
again among the Mysteries. Tremendous

and trembling. It has been over a year
since I heard my brother's voice,
since he stood in the doorway with a knife
in his hands, since he sent the picture
with a gun to his head,
daring a devil only he could see.
We prayed so much in those days,
those days when the last green promises
of spring-song rotted on the vine. We pray
now too, in the Eagles Lodge where the
meetings are held, in the churches it's easy
to make fun of. Tragedy rattles us, rouses us
in a way that beauty may well be jealous
of. Have we ever known what to do
with all these things that never

grew? The children learn our habits.
They gasp at the fawn in the meadow and
tiptoe over, whispering with glee,
"she's looking at me!" and ask to skip rocks
in the creek where the steelhead trout lay
their eggs. Sometimes at night, they rage
in their sleep. There is as much to hold
as to behold in the churning of the generations
and the blink between fifteen and fifty.

One auntie leaves her husband, and the other
doesn't. The new dog is named after the old one.
When there are too many empty bottles
at the family gathering, I go out walking alone in the rain.
It stays green here all year. There are always geraniums
in bloom. The puddles turn the sky into drinkable light.

BLOODLINES

Vicki was the first to get her period, but we didn't know. What is it like to be given the lead, especially one you weren't particularly interested in taking? We spread rumors about why she wouldn't get in the hot tub at the hotel in Montreal. Our faces were steamed pink. We repeated jokes about sex that none of us understood. When she confronted us with a surprisingly mature biological explanation, we laughed uncomfortably. Who else dreamed about blood rivers that night?

I heard that you weren't supposed to work out when you got your period. Or maybe I'd heard that people could tell you were wearing a pad when you had gym shorts on, that it would give you diaper butt, and they would be grossed out. But that cute boy was supposed to be staffing the front desk that day. He used Sun In to bleach his hair and wore cargo shorts with pockets so big I could fit most of my dreams in them. Rachel helped me cover the tampon applicator in Vaseline, coached me on how to insert it. *No one will know now.* Sit-ups. Crunches. Push-ups. Light jog. It didn't feel right. I went home, pulled the plug, and cried into my floral bedsheets.

It is known that Savannah free bleeds. Really, though, it is known that she is free. She sings like a mountain casting off a thick mist and wears whatever she wants. Her freckles are constellations so bold that if you look carefully enough, you can read your whole future on her face. I first met her when she was fifteen. We were reading a Shuntaro Tanikawa poem, and she decided it was fine to stand out from the crowd, even if it made other people uncomfortable.

Iman spent a week sewing reusable cotton and flannel pads to send to a non-profit in sub-Saharan Africa. Can you imagine not being able to go to school because your moon-body needed to take a walk down to earth? I wonder what rituals around this crimson honey have been lost, left behind, dislocated, unlanded. Iman's father came here with soul-screams and bone-sighs and different memories of bloodshed. Their minds clash. At Eid a few years back, she said she couldn't pray because she was on her period. *Is that what you really believe?* She covered her head and started to recite.

At the lip of the creek, I kneel down and spill my cup onto the ground. I swish my bandana in the water and scrub it against the gravel. An older teacher once told me that blood is the most spiritual form of matter. I think of Jesus on the cross. I think of the bobcat born just days ago. Does everything on the inside eventually make its way out? Is the earth the only thing big enough to receive it all?

7

Joan paced around the office, waiting for her period to come. *Please don't be pregnant, please don't be pregnant.* Relief at the blood in the toilet. Megan paced up and down the hallway of her starter home, praying her period wouldn't come. *Please be pregnant, please be pregnant.* Devastation at the blood in her pajamas. As soon as I night-weaned my child, my period returned. My mother got a hysterectomy and couldn't walk for a month. Her unused pads heaped on top of the junk mail in the trash. We are all wading through brackish waters. Our bodies are the roots we trip on. Our bodies are the bridges we use to get across.

Eli cries when he gets his period and refuses to come to school. Once, he locked himself in the car and wouldn't come out until the blood was gone. The endurance of a body swells in proportion to the spirit. What about when the spirit cannot fit in the body? Camellia blossoms fell all around him, and he dreamed himself into a sketchbook where he could be pink and soft and would no longer need to question the seasons. His parents think the pill caused him to have seizures. We are all learning what is true.

The paper is thin and flecked with pulp. Nammy's chapbook slumbers on my desk. She wrote about ghosts and tenderness. She wrote an ode to menstruation. In this world where easy is a marketing ploy and affections come and go with the traffic, she lavishes love on her body, the hard way. Which is to say the real way. Which is also to say, she thinks she's doing it wrong. We're perhaps too familiar with our own blood, the two of us, and we still write to each other in red ink.

The door has been locked, and Nina goes home. She had to turn many women away. No more diapers, no more feminine products. First it was the formula, and now this. She cries at the immensity of the need in the world, at the crookedness of our systems. She connects to her own infinity. *You are vast,* she tells herself. Still, on the bathroom scale, she weighs herself again, trying not to be obsessive. She takes off all her clothes, relieved that the number dips a little. A small drop of blood trickles down her thigh and lands on the 7's shoulder. Isn't this more than a story about losses and gains?

HOW TO GREET A HYPOCRITE

tell stories about weddings
& fig trees
write nothing down
unless with a stick
in the sand

wait for the hosannas to die
down; such earth-bound enthusiasm
will soon exhaust itself
in silence & silence
is necessary

feel the river in your body,
the one you were born in
& splash in what you can never
hold in your hand

what was true at the beginning?
light & darkness & labor &
destruction & striving:
say that

condense the fear into a ball,
a marble you can hold
under your tongue
swallow everything else whole,
but let the body dissolve
that fear

put on your bridegroom's
garments & dance
your movement on the roof
of the world in the sun
of your skin is a perpetually
relevant message

SOMETIMES

I hear that sometimes a person can
pour out all the bottles and flush
all those spirits
down the toilet, never buy another one
not ever again, even on
New Year's Eve.
I hear that sometimes a person can decide
not to strike the match, not to chase the smoke,
for the sake of love or whatever mysterious substance
hearts are actually made of,
and instead find fire everywhere else in
the vicious freedom of
an unadorned life.

But sometimes, like this time,
his sobriety walked out the door,
like his wife eventually did,
and didn't come back.
The bottle and the pop
top and the handle
of a fifth
and the drag of a sticky leaf
and the drone of the daily dying,
not bullets but shots,
pulled him into
some place I can't find on
the only map he left behind.

IT'S NOT A RACE

We run past the bungalow with the blue shutters where I grew up
and learned that safety is relative and love has more hands than the ones

that wrap the towel around a shivering body and fry the bologna and
reach for the paddle because no one ever taught them otherwise. We run

past the field where proud Black bodies perform calisthenics and I think
of Grace and her red barrettes in Mr. Halowicki's gym class. We run past

dueling flags that proclaim which lives matter and boarded up liquor shops
and the motel my dad said the prostitutes lived in but I don't know if I

believe that and now there is an allotment garden out back with towering
sunflowers and bean tendrils spiraling themselves up to the sky. We run

into women mowing lawns who say hello and women chatting on porches
who say hello and a man washing his car who does not but we greet him anyway.

We don't know anyone here now, but we know the houses and too many
of the stories they hold in their bones. The real estate trends say white flight,

and yes, where I am, flying through the streets where I don't belong but
maybe could, trying to understand with each pavement strike what it means

to be from a place where there was still a dirt road behind the Methodist church,
where racial slurs were common parlance, and where I was taught to be white.

I run deeper into a history I haven't learned how to hold, into envy for those
who can own a home, who rebuilt this neighborhood when abandoning it

was the obvious option, when the meager but not insignificant privilege
packed its bags and went looking for larger lawns and a two-car garage.

We don't run past the Lebanese bakery where Salem Haddad's family bought
their bread or the factory where my father worked nights with his bare hands in

industrial ink we never thought twice about until he got cancer. We circle
back again to the blue shutters, to grandma's house next door. She's dead,

grandpa's dead, but the house has a fresh coat of paint and geraniums
in the planter box. I roller skated in that driveway and weeded the rose garden.

The house was always clean and tidy. We wipe our sweat. It starts to rain, and the sky stutters and sobs all over our bodies. Every breath is heavy with

memory, heavy with whatever it is we can still feel but will never understand. We run until my dad says he's done but then decide to take one more lap

around the neighborhood to see what else we've forgotten to remember.

MISSING MONARCHY

1.
There is a natural intimacy
between earth and sky
that the wing-beings are trying
to whisper to us. Where
is the quiet that will let me hear?

2.
Beside the small soda spring
where the bubbling water tastes of blood
and we streak our faces with red-
orange clay, a student hands me
a wing of a monarch butterfly.
I feel like this is something
you'd want to touch, she says,
and she is right. Quite like a feather,
soft and miraculous.

3.
We plant milkweed and cosmos.
Then marigold and aster. We wait.
This is a kind of prayer.

4.
The buddleias of her memory
have all dried up in the summer
haze. Sun unrelenting. We were almost
on a quest for purple. What's left
of their small petals turns
to dust between my fingers.
The butterflies that once feasted
here have not moved on,
they are simply gone. Loving
in this world entails significant
grief.

5.
I stand in front of a mural
in Pacific Grove. Black and orange
fan out like my two hands, open,
asking, in all this confusion, what

can remain? Hubris wants us
to be saviors. Humility wants us
to be a part of Every Thing
that is saving itself.

REVOLUTIONS IN MEANING

1a. an orbital motion about a point, esp. as distinguished from an axial rotation

The dictionary cannot make visible to me the difference between orbital and axial. I wonder if she could. I wonder if she could hold something in her hands, cast it in the role of a lifetime as The Great Turning, and take no credit for having directed this cosmic spectacle. She is not here now though. I scour the diagrams, static images on a screen of what is meant to be in motion, what cannot possibly stand still, ask my eyes to extend the movement of the arrows from their two-dimensional depiction and into my three-dimensional life. I cross-reference astronomical explanations and charts and equations with variables I have never encountered. What else have I never encountered? I vaguely grasp that one can be moving forward while still being pulled back— or is it elsewhere or is it away? I timidly allow my body to feel its own orbital path. Can I call it a revolution?

1b. A turning or rotational motion about an axis

I picture a carnival ride, the teacups. The grimy wheel in the center. The built-in bench that goes all the way around the inside, perfect for sliding. Gather your friends, hand over your tickets, it's time to twirl. Mechanical belching. Achy and overused joints of the machinery screech to life, give a little jolt. The cups, outstretched on tentacular metal arms, start to rotate like the second hand on a clock, jumpy for just a moment, then smooth. Some kind of column in the middle that tethers us all together, the center around which we spin. It would have been enough to just circle like this, but carnivals are not for subtlety or leaving well enough alone. Hands hit the wheel and crank, unlicensed and reckless drivers on a non-existent road. A second kind of rotation splishes and splashes the bodies inside the mirthful teacup. Clockwise, counterclockwise, switching at any moment. One revolution after another, spinning spinning spinning, until someone yells stop. I was always the one who yelled stop. I was always the one who couldn't stand steady on solid ground after the dismount.

1c. A single complete cycle of such orbital or axial motion

I formed each from the inside, stood enclosed by my creation. One rock at a time, the fire pit emerged from my effort. One rock at a time, the medicine wheel birthed itself through my body. One rock at a time, the altar woven with sky and sand through my hands. One rock at a time, the zero held its ground and signaled the end of the countdown. There is no more waiting. The revolution is here.

2. The overthrow and replacement of a government

Which versions are real? The unfolding of events that can't be tucked back into the envelope. The revolutionary breath that can't be put back into King's lungs. Gandhi bowing at the crowd as he went down. Spirits that can't be incarcerated belonging to bodies that can. Laulupidu because words are weapons and songs are slick cannonballs slicing through the air. Dessalines carrying out the last days of the scorched earth campaign. Freedom fires lick the world back into its wild. The Republic's renaming of the months while there was still blood on the cobblestones of the public square. There is still blood in the public square. Who showed up and why? Who is interviewing the human heart, recording its rhythms and skipped beats, playing back its testimony on the evening news, as evidence that there are still revolutions we can't not believe in?

3. A sudden or momentous change in situation

Yesterday I had hair; today I have stubble. This morning, I hung the damp clothes out on the balcony, and this afternoon they are dry; at what moment did they cross over? As a teenager, I snuck out of the hotel room on 42nd Street and wrote about never wanting to marry or have children or need other human beings; these days I reside in the whorl of these universes of relationality. Under an absurdly blue sky on Montara Mountain, I promised myself to never miss another panorama; how many days, like today, have I chosen to stay under the covers? Once, for the longest once, I feared my own body, other bodies, all bodies, any body, everybody; then I didn't. In fact, right this very moment, I summon my desire and my dry bones rise up to fight for what they were fearfully and wonderfully made to feel. Are any of these revolutions? I don't know what it means to see something as sudden or momentous when my eyes are forged out of such aeons.

4. *Geology* A time of major crustal deformation, when folds and faults are formed

Would you read articles written in the 1830s about the moral and religious truths contained in the earth's strata? Samuel Metcalf was trying to find his way past the commercial extraction of valuable resources. Geology traced a new fault line between the mineral and the almighty. All along, every atom, whether from the flax and the chaff or the volcanic crust, has been speaking out of deep time. Anyone who hears recapitulates the revolution, is shaped into something new.

THIRST

I rushed through
the Châtelet station
with all the others,
sped across the moving walkway
in sync with the crowd.
I saw a mother struggle
with her bulky stroller
and a gray-bearded man
in a djellaba clinging
to the handrail
as commuters shoved their way
through. I didn't slow down.

I snaked my way
toward the table
with all the others.
We always assumed there
would be enough, if not
more. I loaded my plate
like everyone else. Roasted
potatoes and fresh berries.
I went for seconds. Grilled
asparagus, key lime pie.
I ate more than my fill. I wrote
a thank you note to the waiter
on the back of the receipt, but
the bus boy cleared it, along
with enough leftovers
from my fellow diners to
feed many hungry men.

I stood in line
on the lip of the curb
with all the others.
When it started to rain,
I opened my umbrella
& asked my neighbor
if she wanted to duck
under with me. She smiled,
said yes. We didn't speak
beyond that moment.

I watched a few others rehearse
this delicate ritual.
I watched many more
undefended against the downpour.

In the end, like the others, I have
sometimes thirsted for goodness,
and sometimes I have pursed my lips
and turned away. Aren't we all
always of at least two hearts?

A BIKE COMMUTER'S MODEST USE OF DEMOCRACY

Dear civil servant, this message is addressed to you because
The mornings are so precarious: finger clouds are
Scratching the sky and hoarfrost cloaks wrap the
Black earth
Yes, yes, of course this is not your purview
But context can be a heartening thing for
Those of us who do not take the roads armored
Commandeering large vessels
Relying on satellite navigational systems in an attempt to outsmart
The trail of marching
Red ants inching toward the next intersection, so as you read on
Remember
We take it on our cheeks, me and my kin
We take it in our lungs, it burns sometimes
Both the rime and the coughing barges
But boldly do we go in our thirteen inches of not-quite-ditch
Using sleepy muscles and keen seeing and hoping our
Phosphorescent vests are enough to
Keep from not existing at the strike of some ungodly Continental
Tread
You see, the city has a workforce I'm told, brooms and callused hands and care
for
Common welfare and pride in what We can do
So what can we do
About this narrow runway from which our spokes and such never take off
Rather just keep landing one revolution after another
Over backwashed and persistent debris
(the wind has been throwing tantrums in her old age, not unlike those
small, sweet-cheeked creatures that have been strapped in styrofoam-lined seats
of my racing passersby)
Between you and me, I have only just learned to balance
I have only just found my pace
What I am asking for is some help staying safe

MOVING ON

I wrap the framed photograph of the Garden of Gethsemane
in a fleece blanket, secure it with remnants of yarn. I do the same
with the Van Gogh poster, the canvas print of my daughter
and niece running into a summer sunset. I layer the few

ceramic plates with washcloths and wrap the mugs in dish towels.
We save money this way, and spare the trash bin too. A man
I admire says to leave it all and buy what we need when we get there.
He says the cost of labor alone is more than what it would take

to stock the kitchen secondhand, find a desk, a couch. But his calculations
fail to account for the fact that the labor is mine, the hours mine, the heave
and heft mine, and the pay nothing more than a chance to touch a few raw
memories one last time before saying goodbye. Parallel lines of light stripe

the bedroom floor. My younger daughter was born here, beside the balcony,
from my belly to my arms to my bed in one miraculous breath. We *lived*
here. Every evening, no matter the weather, the hills are coated in honey-shine.
The laundry hung out to dry, while days became years. A kitchen full

of neighborhood children, batches of blueberry muffins with lemon zest,
cheaper than store-bought, and we all pass the bowl around to lick
clean what's left of the batter. Simple pleasures for pennies. Flatbreads
frying in smoking oil. Green onion cuttings growing back in a jar on the shelf.
The landlord comes to negotiate our exit, part of a greater exodus.
You're right to get out. It's time you bought a place of your own,
as his wife takes our money and deducts for the stains in the carpet. I teach
to fill my heart, not my pocketbook, I joke, and we've been on a single income

since the start of the pandemic. My dad dreams of going halves on a house
on a lake where we spend our summers, where we gather for Christmas,
where we keep the radio tuned to a station that plays Cat Stevens. It would
be nice, I think, as I put down the security deposit and first month's rent,

a full month's salary, on our new rental. There's a small cluster of redwood trees
in the sliver of space off the bedroom. The American River's a walk away. I don't
know what it means to be borrowing my way through this world full of grief and
exuberance, but I turn my ears to what the trees have to say about home.

CELEBRATIONS
for and with Nammy

This is a day to celebrate scotch
tape dispensers, those exoskeletal spool
stores with tiny jagged plastic teeth
that have of late replaced the ferocious
metal fangs of old
indiscriminately doling out almost opaque
ribbon (that takes upon itself my fingerprint
before) it binds the page of *Atlas of a Difficult World*
that would otherwise have been lost and
affixes on the stucco walls a single sepia
memory
of the summer
before the Arab Spring

Today let us bless the late train
the slumbering steel giant not yet lumbering
into the overwhelmed station
with my soured brow I can't be coaxed to
wait without consulting the obtuse timetable
unlaminated underappreciated
and scan the platform for signs of mechanical life
instead a run appears in the stockings on an
exquisite leg follow those unassuming tracks
instead spend time on that trajectory instead it is going
somewhere without a clock

Today let us exalt the briefest of
communions, olive tree branching into sky
your hand slipping into mine
flickering aeroplane lights within
distant earthbound eyes
slender breastbone muffling
her thirsty infant's cries
and the moonlit rivulets returning desperately
between archipelagos of footprinted sand
to salty high tides under pregnant nights

Today let us venerate long distance
phone-calls, staticky lines
that almost convey the glow of your voice

the carved wooden box full of careworn letters
written decades ago, slightly yellowed within
her bedside table
crowds of patient halves waiting
in airport gates, cardboard signs saying
"thank god, you're home"

Today let me thank the creaking steps
leading to your open front door,
where nostalgia and maddening traffic
end with your eyes boring into my core
and here at last are you, old friend
weathered by life perhaps,
but radiating warmth that
has only grown
with time

Alison Davis is a lifelong student who was born in Detroit, Michigan, lives in California, and explores the world through teaching and learning. Her literary work engages the qualities of devotion and awe, which are equally available in both joy and in grief, in the everyday and in the extraordinary. As a scholar, Alison's research focuses on participatory pedagogy, spiritual inquiry, and healing practices. As a human being who believes in interconnection and deep relationality, Alison's social justice work, especially in food justice, embodies the transformative paradigm as a path of mutual liberation. She likes lists, litanies, and alliteration. She loves making trash art with her kids, running up mountains (both real and imagined), and praying to the God of her understanding.